HOW TO
Teach Effectively

HOW TO

Teach Effectively

A BRIEF GUIDE
SECOND EDITION

BRUCE D. FRIEDMAN
California State University, Bakersfield

LYCEUM
BOOKS, INC.

Chicago, Illinois

© 2013 by Lyceum Books, Inc.

Published by

LYCEUM BOOKS, INC.
5758 S. Blackstone Ave.
Chicago, Illinois 60637
773+643-1903 fax
773+643-1902 phone
lyceum@lyceumbooks.com
www.lyceumbooks.com

6 5 4 3 2 1   13 14 15 16 17

ISBN 978-1-935871-28-6

Printed in the United States of America.

Library of Congress Cataloging-in-Publication Data

Friedman, Bruce D., 1952–
   How to teach effectively : a brief guide / Bruce D. Friedman, California State University, Bakersfield.—Second edition.
     pages cm
   Includes bibliographical references.
   ISBN 978-1-935871-28-6 (pbk. : alk. paper)
  1. Effective teaching. I. Title.
  LB1025.3.F765   2013
  371.102—dc23

                                               2012033498

THIS GUIDE IS A PRODUCT OF LOVE, and I dedicate it to the people who most influenced that love: to my father, the ultimate teacher, may he rest in peace, whose unconditional love encouraged me to continually strive to improve myself and to give to others even when there may be nothing given in return; to my sons, Jaron and Bryan, with whom I learned to give of myself, selflessly; and, of course, to Rosalie, from whom I learned the meaning of giving unconditional love.

CONTENTS

Preface ix

Acknowledgments xiii

Part I: Teaching and Learning Styles 1

Introduction 2

Teaching Styles 3

Adult Learning Styles 4

Types of Learners 6

Types of Learning 8

Moving from Passive Learning to Active Learning 12

Factors Affecting Learning 16

Part II: Tools and Techniques 19

Tools 20

Visual Aids 27

Room Set-Up 30

Training Methods 31

Active Discussion Tools and Techniques 35

Techniques to Encourage Good Discussion 40

Be Prepared for Difficult Participants 45

Your Personal Style 49

Conclusion 50

Recommended Readings 51

References 53

PREFACE

OVER THE COURSE OF MY LIFE, I have learned that teachers do not become teachers because of their ability to teach, but rather because they have some knowledge of a subject. All teachers need help and guidance as we face the challenge of transmitting our knowledge and experience to learners in order to help them develop understanding and mastery of a subject.

I remember teaching my first university class, a class on social work practice with families. On the first day of class, after asking the students to arrange their chairs in a circle, I was dismayed to see them writing down every word I said as though it were gospel. After class, I went to the office of the chair of the department and shared my experience with him. His response was, "You are a social worker; you will figure it out." Well, I have been working at figuring it out.

How to Teach Effectively represents my accumulated knowledge and skills: it is a guide that blends the adult learning principles recommended by social worker Malcolm Knowles with the methods of collaborative educational processes in order to create an active learning environment. It is also a guide to integrating technology into the learning environment; the way students learn has changed over the years, and students have become more astute in their use of technology. It is a guide to thinking through what you, as the teacher, want to accomplish, and it is a guide to designing a course, including the evaluation mechanisms, to enhance the classroom experience for you and your students.

Instead of writing lengthy text for the guide, I have opted for a format similar to that of a training manual that uses short lists and highlights essential points. I find that the pace of our lifestyle is so hurried that many people feel that they do not have time to read, and prefer to skim through documents for the highlights. Therefore, this guide is designed so that you will be able to find what you need without spending a lot of time reading nonessential content. The bulleted points should make the content readily accessible, usable, and easy to apply.

The reality of your role as a teacher is that you are not in a classroom just to provide information—most people believe they can gain that from a book—but to create a learning environment in which learners sense the value of being present. It is just as important to create the experience as it is to transmit the information. Learners today are sophisticated in their ability to search for information, but they are not as sophisticated in their knowledge of how to properly use and apply the information. Thus, creating the classroom experience means not only presenting knowledge, but also introducing affective and psychomotor learning. If you are able to integrate these types of learning into the classroom experience, you will provide your learners with an enhanced understanding of the information, and you will create a sense of community that will make your learners recognize the value of attending classes. This guide provides overviews of each of the different types of learning and descriptions of how to use them to create a more effective learning environment.

A quick word about evaluation: accrediting organizations are concerned with how we assess and evaluate learners' understanding of what we teach. On the one hand, we can state objectives at the beginning of the course and then use a variety of methods to test whether we have successfully achieved those objectives. It is important to understand how we formulate those objectives, however. Did we focus our teaching methods on a single learning style, like cognitive learning, and then use quantified tests that learners crammed for the night before? How did that style lend itself to the focus of the class? My experience has been that focusing my teaching solely on a cognitive learning style creates an environment in which the teacher is the expert and the focus of the class. In this kind of environment, the learners hang on to the teacher's every word because they are concerned about regurgitating that exact content for an exam. In the past, the use of this kind of teaching style allowed medical students to substitute tape recorders for their actual presence in lecture courses.

On the other hand, evaluation is part of the process of gaining critical thinking skills—that is, the ability to integrate cognitive knowledge into demonstrated skills. Thus, it is clear that our most important goal is to create an environment that encourages critical thinking. In such an environment, the teacher is no longer the "sage on the stage" but rather the "guide on the side" (Friedman, Ward, & Biagianti, 1998). Evaluation becomes a process of thinking and writing rather than performing well on a quantified exam. I remember, as a student, getting a paper back from a professor and flipping to the last page for the grade, ignoring the comments that the professor had written throughout the paper. What did I learn from that? It was not until I looked at the comments and tried to integrate the comments and the content that learning took place for me. Now, as a professor, I require my learners to revise and resubmit their assignments. This creates a more interactive evaluation process: students learn by continuing to do and redo until they have the concept down. This creates a training model within a classroom setting. It also creates opportunities for sharing and building knowledge; the focus of the class becomes building knowledge and thinking rather than regurgitating the words of the instructor. Sure, it may be a little more work for the teacher, but the work is part of our job and part of our commitment to enhance critical-thinking processes in the classroom. Integrating affective learning into the classroom experience leads to a change of focus from the front of the classroom to the entire classroom.

How to Teach Effectively provides you with the basic tools you will need to get started creating an active-learning critical-thinking environment. It provides some information on cognitive learning, describes affective learning and the rationale for using it, and gives you the psychomotor tools that you can use immediately to make affective learning happen. It also provides an opportunity for you to do some self-exploration regarding your own learning style. I have found that we teach the way we were taught. Unless we make a conscious effort to understand the strengths and weaknesses of our own learning styles, we cannot be sensitive to the way others learn, which we must be since we do not all learn in the same way. Understanding your learning and teaching styles will make you better able to adapt your teaching to address other people's learning patterns. This guide provides a strategy for understanding each person's learning style.

How to Teach Effectively also offers a few basic tips on using technology and integrating it into the classroom experience. Because technology changes rapidly, these tips are not exhaustive but rather are a building block for the future. They are a foundation for understanding the rudiments of teaching with technology, which you can then personalize and develop to suit your personal teaching style.

I begin this guide with a quote attributed to Confucius, a simple message that reminds us that learning is more than a passive process—it is an active one. It is important that as we continue to grow and develop as teachers, we think about how to make learning more active. Many people think that there is an art to teaching, but there is also a scientific process. *How to Teach*

Effectively helps you identify your own artistic strengths and then provides some scientific tools that will help you build on your artistic ability. It is up to you to utilize these tools, to personalize them, and to integrate them into your own art form, where your classroom is the canvas. This guide can be the beginning of your shift from teaching within a passive environment to creating an active learning experience for the learners.

ACKNOWLEDGMENTS

THIS GUIDE IS A PRODUCT OF MY YEARS on the faculty at the College of Osteopathic Medicine at Michigan State University, where I began to develop the knowledge and skills of collaborative cooperative education utilizing adult learning principles; at the University of Texas Pan American; and at California State University Bakersfield. I would like to thank my colleagues from the College of Osteopathic Medicine who are now dispersed throughout the world: Karen, Sandro, Kathy, Eileen, Dan, and, of course, the many fellows and academic physician leaders with whom I initially tested these concepts as they were going through their respective programs. I would also like to thank Karen for our work together on affective learning.

PART I

Teaching and Learning Styles

What I hear, I forget.
What I see, I remember.
What I do, I understand.
—Confucius

INTRODUCTION

How to Teach Effectively provides an overview of instructional theory and describes techniques that you as a teacher can use when presenting course content. The emphasis is on utilizing adult learning theory and collaborative cooperative learning techniques to provide instruction that meets the educational needs of adult learners. Using these materials, you will be able to do the following:

I Identify positive and negative learning situations.
I Describe the difference between adult-to-child and adult-to-adult teaching styles.
I Understand the various ways in which individuals learn.
I Understand the difference between passive and active learning.
I Identify factors that influence learning.
I Improve learning through enhanced teaching skills.
I Understand how your personal teaching style can influence the educational experience.

Part I of this guide focuses on the ways that people learn; explores what can make the process more enjoyable, effective, and efficient; and offers helpful hints for providing a successful educational experience. This essential information helps teachers maximize information and skill transfer from a classroom setting to real practice situations. The way information is transferred is often as important as the information itself.

The challenge is to maximize information transfer while utilizing the best instructional methods to maximize retention. This becomes an even greater challenge when you are presenting information within a technology environment, such as on the web or through interactive television, since much of the learning is done on an individual basis already and is not supported by the interactions that take place in a classroom setting.

TEACHING STYLES

Most of us build on our experiences as learners when we try to teach others. As students, we were most familiar with an adult-to-child teaching style. The components of that style are the following:

I Teacher decides what the learners should learn.
I Teacher and learner both see education as a one-way street.
I Teacher minimizes the value of the learner's experiences.
I Teacher and learner both see learner as an empty vessel and teacher as a full vessel.

The adult-to-child teaching style creates an image of the teacher as the sage on the stage and fosters a passive learning modality for learners. To begin to make the change from creating a passive learning environment to fostering an active learning environment, you must begin to focus on the characteristics of the learner rather than yourself as the teacher. Biggs (Biggs & Tang, 2011) calls this "constructive alignment." It relies on the instructor understanding how the learner learns and engaging the learner at his or her level of understanding. There are a number of adult learning principles that you can incorporate to achieve this refocus:

I The learner negotiates with the teacher what the teacher will teach and the learner will learn.
I The educational experience becomes a give-and-take relationship between teacher and learner.
I The teacher acknowledges that each learner has an educational background and experiences that influence his or her learning.
I The teacher and the learner share information.

These principles create the image of the teacher as the guide on the side and foster an active learning modality for the learner.

ADULT LEARNING STYLES

As you begin to understand learning and teaching styles, keep in mind the following key adult learning principles:

I Adults are self-directed.

I Adults need to know why they need to learn.

I Adults appreciate being involved in setting their own learning objectives.

I Adults prefer to learn in an environment characterized by mutual trust, respect, and freedom of expression.

I Adults learn from their own experiences and the experiences of others.

I Adults prefer to acquire knowledge they can apply immediately.

I Adults learn better when they are actively involved in the learning process. Adults like to be involved in evaluating their progress toward the achievement of their goals (Knowles, 1980).

To integrate these principles into your teaching experience, it is important to engage learners from the beginning. To do this, you can start with an exercise that helps the learners begin to think about the content and information they are about to learn and the importance of learning it, and that allows learners to build on their own learning experiences.

Exercise: Positive and Negative Learning Experiences

Ask your learners to think about an exemplary learning experience. Who was teaching or facilitating? What made the experience so positive? After they have had time to think about this, ask them to describe the experience on one side of a folded sheet of paper. Next, ask your learners to think about their worst learning experience. Who was teaching or facilitating? What made the experience so negative? After they have had time to think about this, have them describe the experience on the other side of the paper.

After your learners have written their responses, ask volunteers to share their best experiences. Have a learner help by listing or summarizing characteristics of the experiences on a flipchart or blackboard. After a few people have shared their experiences, ask if there are any other positive learning characteristics that have not been listed. Summarize this portion of the exercise and seek consensus on what makes a learning experience positive.

Follow this process by discussing learners' worst experiences. As before, summarize the responses and seek consensus on the factors that make a learning experience negative. Identify common themes that show up on both lists: respect (or lack thereof), engagement (or lack of engagement) in the learning experience, and so on. Identify any outstanding teaching styles that positively affected the participants. It is important for you as a teacher to understand that the way you learn will influence the way that you present the information. If you become aware of your own learning style, then it is possible to realize that is how you will be presenting the information. Only then will you be able to recognize and introduce alternative methods to address the various other learning styles of the learners in the class.

How Learning Takes Place

Figure 1 illustrates how learning takes place. As teachers, we often integrate our learning to such a degree that much of what we do becomes automatic and we do not consciously think about the steps that we take to perform the skills that we need in order to do our jobs. Most of our learners come to class not knowing what they need to know: this is unconscious incompetence. As they begin to gain understanding, they begin to learn what they do not know: this is conscious incompetence. We teach them the skills they need to become competent in their respective professional areas of growth and development: this is conscious competence. The more proficient they become and the more they develop those skills, the more automatic their actions will become and the less they will need

FIGURE 1 – How Learning Takes Place

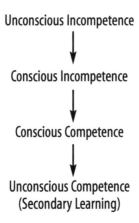

Unconscious Incompetence

Conscious Incompetence

Conscious Competence

Unconscious Competence
(Secondary Learning)

to think through the steps to do them; this is unconscious competence or secondary learning.

TYPES OF LEARNERS

To understand how to move from passive to active learning, it is important to understand the different types of learners. There are four primary learning styles: visual, auditory, read-write, and kinesthetic. People learn using a variety of these methods, but one method usually predominates. Familiarity with the characteristics of each learning style and associated strategies allows you to address the needs of each type of learner. Have your learners go to www.vark-learn.com and complete the questionnaire to learn what type of learner they are. By having them share this information with you, you can begin to adapt to their preferred learning style.

Visual Learners

Visual learners are characterized by the following:

∎ They tend to be fast talkers.
∎ They exhibit impatience and have a tendency to interrupt.

I They use words and phrases that evoke visual images.

I They learn by seeing and visualizing.

Your teaching strategy for visual learners should include the use of demonstrations and visually pleasing materials, and you should make an effort to paint mental pictures for these learners.

Auditory Learners

Auditory learners are characterized by the following:

I They speak slowly and tend to be natural listeners.

I They think in a linear manner.

I They prefer to have things explained to them orally rather than to read written information.

I They learn by listening and verbalizing.

Your teaching strategy for auditory learners should be planned and delivered in the form of an organized conversation.

Read-Write Learners

Read-write learners are characterized by the following:

I They prefer information to be displayed in writing, such as lists of ideas.

I They emphasize text-based input and output.

I They enjoy reading and writing in all forms.

Your teaching strategy for read-write learners should include written lists of key words. The learners will learn by silently reading or rewriting their notes repeatedly; writing out in their own words the ideas and principles that were taught or discussed; organizing any diagrams, graphs, other visual depictions into statements (e.g., "The trend is . . ."); and putting reactions, actions, diagrams, charts, and flowcharts into words. These learners like multiple-choice tests.

Kinesthetic Learners

Kinesthetic learners are characterized by the following:

I They tend to be the slowest talkers of all.
I They tend to be slow to make decisions.
I They use all their senses to engage in learning.
I They learn by doing and solving real-life problems.
I They like hands-on approaches and learn through trial and error.

Your teaching strategy for kinesthetic learners should include hands-on demonstrations and case examples to be discussed and solved.

Can You Identify Your Predominant Learning Style?

There are a variety of types of learners in a single classroom, which means teachers need to use a number of learning styles during a class period. Therefore, it is important to incorporate multiple teaching methods. It is also important to know your own predominant learning style, because when you teach you may unintentionally favor your learning style and shortchange other types of learners in the classroom.

TYPES OF LEARNING

In order to enhance the learning experience, it is also important to identify and understand the types of learning you are striving to cover: cognitive, affective, or psychomotor. As you design a lesson plan, you should identify the goal of the learning and which of the learning types you will address. (Remember, the goal may be to cover more than one of the types of learning.) One size does not fit all, and it is important to incorporate activities that recognize multiple learning types into each classroom session. By identifying the type of learning that you intend to cover, it will be possible for you to develop an appropriate assessment plan to measure the effectiveness of the session.

Cognitive Learning

Cognitive learning is a form of building knowledge about a subject. Bloom (1956) identified six levels of cognition within cognitive learning (see figure 2). It is easy to emphasize the lower-order levels, but it is important for learners to progress to higher-order levels, which enhance critical-thinking skills.

FIGURE 2 – Cognitive Learning

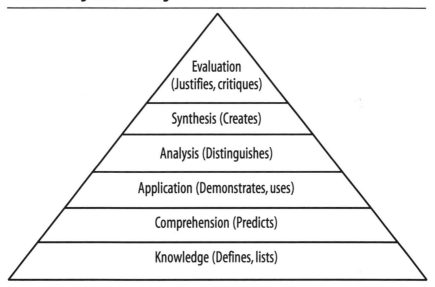

Assessing Cognitive Learning

Most quantitative tests are good measures of assessing cognitive learning. Use of multiple-choice questions can demonstrate whether the learner has the basic knowledge of the content. However, does it measure higher-order cognitive learning based on Bloom's Taxonomy? One way to reach the higher-order levels is to develop a case example with multiple choices, similar to what the licensing exams do. In this manner, you are asking the learner to analyze the case and then synthesize the best answer from those provided. Hence, case-based learning is a good way to assess higher-level cognitive learning.

Affective Learning

Krathwohl (1964, 1993) was one of the first scholars to look at learning as acquiring not just cognition, but also values (see figure 3). Much of what a teacher presents in the classroom has a value orientation. If a learner does not see the relevance or value of a subject, it is harder for him or her to integrate the content. For example, many learners in the social sciences have an aversion to math and question why they need to take college algebra in order to complete their general education requirements. The instructor focuses on obtaining the correct answer rather than on the rationale behind the algebraic formula. Getting the right answer is cognitive learning, whereas understanding the theory behind the formula is affective learning. A teacher who emphasizes the value and relevance of algebra might discuss the difference between math and arithmetic. Once learners understand that math is the theory or the rationale behind the action of doing, whereas, arithmetic is about the numbers, it is easier for the learner to see the value of algebra, since algebra is more about theory

FIGURE 3 – Neuman's Taxonomy on Affective Learning

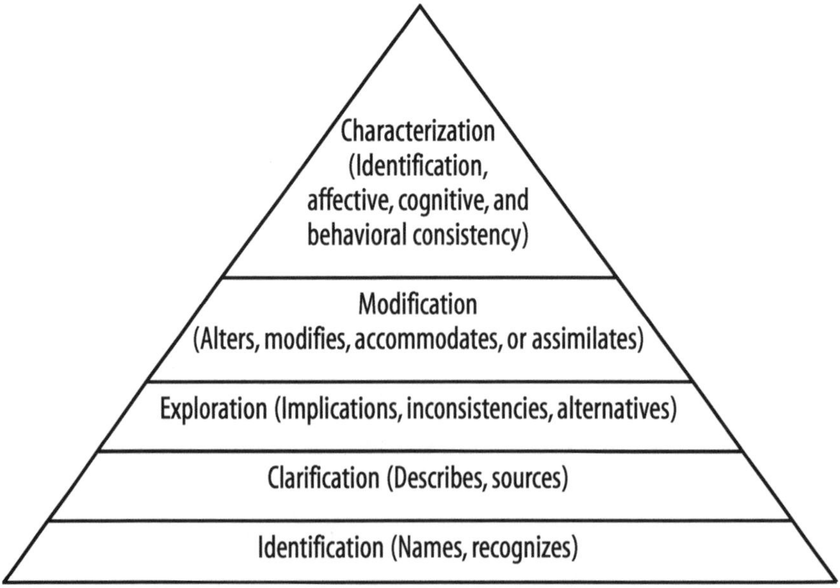

Characterization
(Identification,
affective, cognitive, and
behavioral consistency)

Modification
(Alters, modifies, accommodates, or assimilates)

Exploration (Implications, inconsistencies, alternatives)

Clarification (Describes, sources)

Identification (Names, recognizes)

Source: Allen & Friedman, 2010.

than it is about numbers. When you present content, it is important to integrate an affective component into that presentation; this explains why it is important to learn that content satisfies the need-to-know principle that is characteristic of adult learning.

Neuman and Friedman (2008) modified Krathwohl's original taxonomy assuming that the issue of gaining attention and assuring receptivity and motivation are separate learning concerns that occur in any and all learning situations. Whether teaching for cognitive, behavioral, or affective change, the teacher must employ strategies to get and maintain the students' motivation and attention, which will be identified in part II of this book.

Assessing Affective Learning

Affective learning is one of the more difficult learning styles to assess since the emphasis is on valuing or subjective influencing of the learners (Allen & Friedman, 2010). Thus, we rely on both cognitive and psychomotor learning techniques in order to assess the affective learning domain. However, it is still possible to assess whether affective learning has taken place, since it relies on the ability to adapt the content into one's being. Assessment terms in the affective domain would be "defends," "justifies," "advocates," "argues," "accepts," "challenges," "promotes," "rejects," "shares," "subscribes," "verifies," and "disputes" (Allen & Friedman, 2010). Affective learning involves the learner understanding the content and then using it as a behavioral consistency. Activities such as advocating for a policy change or integrating aspects from the code of ethics would be demonstrations of ways to measure the affective domain. The use of case-based learning with a structured case where the learner must demonstrate an ability to integrate a concept into a practice behavior would be a good measurement of affective learning.

Psychomotor Learning

Psychomotor learning (figure 4) requires learners to demonstrate a particular skill as part of the learning experience. Simpson (1972) realized that there is more than knowledge associated with learning: there are also actions that come from that knowledge. Modeling and apprenticeship experiences, both of which utilize a lower-order skill in psychomotor

FIGURE 4 – Psychomotor Learning

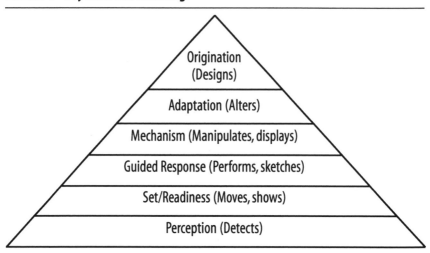

learning, are two forms of psychomotor learning demonstrated early in one's educational career. It is important for the learner to be competent in the skill before he or she can apply it to various situations and create new and improved methods of doing a job, or integrate his or her own style into performing a task.

Assessing Psychomotor Learning

To assess psychomotor learning it is possible to use observation of a skill to ascertain whether the learner can perform it. The use of video or audio tapes can assist in being able to observe skills when the practicum instructor does not have the ability to perform direct supervision. In addition, process records are useful tools in assessing skill level, particularly in the higher levels of adaptation or origination when the learner will have to demonstrate the cognitive knowledge through a skill set when relating to a specific situation.

MOVING FROM PASSIVE LEARNING TO ACTIVE LEARNING

Passive learning is learning in which learners do not have to take an active role. They gain the information through readings, demonstrations, lectures, or interactions between the teacher and other learners. This type of learning is valuable in that it is a quick way of transferring a large amount of information from a teacher to learners. However, there is some concern about whether learners retain information taught in this way. Passive learning is most often linked with memorization and simple fact recall.

Active learning takes place when learners analyze, discuss, debate, or process the information provided by the instructor; link it to relevant activities; or incorporate the information into decision-making processes. Learners may be challenged with a problem or activity that involves debate and resolution. Small groups may be convened to negotiate a solution or to identify how the issue being discussed is relevant to their lives. Actively involving the learner in the learning process is important because adult learners process information better if they can

I Do something with the information,

I Discuss the information with others,

I Ask questions about the information,

I Compare and contrast the information to other information,

I Reflect on the information, and

I Evaluate results.

Recently, student-engaged, active teaching has been identified as "flipping" the classroom to improve teaching (Barrett, 2012). It is useful to identify the types of problems you might encounter if you were teaching in one style to learners who were accustomed to another style. For example, for those who have experienced only passive learning, would the increased responsibility of active learning be stressful? Another way of thinking about this is to focus on the way people learn in different cultures. It is important to be responsive to cultural differences associated with the learning process. For example, at a conference in Mexico at which I presented, the participants were used to having the presenter sit behind a table and lecture for an hour. That was different from the way that I normally present, and when asked by the organizers what I needed, I requested two wireless microphones. At first, there was some confusion as to what I was doing since it was so different from the norm. Only after watching me take the wireless microphones around to different members of the audience for about twenty minutes did they realize that I was not talking *to* them but rather was engaging them in a discussion. Toward the end of the hour, there was so much energy in the room that the conference organizers decided to let us keep going for another hour and to find another location for the session that was to follow. Thus, it is important to be sensitive to culture, but also to realize that one can use active learning as a way to give people permission to talk about their feelings and thoughts.

Can you describe the ideal learning experience? Ideally, teachers should do all of the following as they teach:

- Involve the learner in the learning process.
- Involve the learner in identifying learning goals and objectives.
- Relate the subject matter so that it is relevant to the learner.
- Structure activities so that learners identify solutions to problems.
- Engage learners in high levels of thinking such as analyzing, critiquing, and assessing.
- Utilize a variety of teaching modalities, such as small group process, lecture, and experiential activities.
- Be flexible and meet each learner's needs.
- Provide information that will overlap with information learners already have.
- Reiterate and reinforce information throughout the session.

An active learning process involves listening, demonstrating, interacting, and understanding in order to engage all learners. Adult learners tend to need to interact and share with others. Well-designed training and educational programs use both active and passive methods. There needs to be some information transfer, but information that is shared only in a passive learning format is likely to become boring or seem irrelevant to learners. The key to teaching adults is to provide new information that is relevant and usable within a relatively short period. A good framework to keep in mind is the active training credo:

What I **hear**, I *forget*.

What I hear and **see**, I *remember a little*.

What I hear, see, and **ask questions about** or **discuss** with someone else, I begin to *understand*.

What I hear, see, discuss, and **do**, I *acquire* knowledge and skill.

What I **teach** to another, I *master*. (Silberman, 1996, p. 1)

As a teacher, your goal is not only to present information that learners need, but also to facilitate experiences that will help them gain and master the knowledge and skills that they need to know and practice. By using a variety of teaching techniques and by actively involving learners in the experience, we increase the chances that they will retain and use the information.

I always try to take into consideration what I call the Sesame Street factor. Most Generation X'ers and Millennials grew up on *Sesame Street*, a TV program for children that uses short vignettes that are usually no longer than one or two minutes. Children who watched the early *Sesame Street* episodes are now adults who want their information in short and quick forms. The average adult attention span is between six and twenty minutes, but this varies greatly depending on factors such as the initial interest in the topic, the heat of the room, the time of day, and the energy level of the learner (Johnstone & Percival, 1976; Middendorf & Kalish, 1996). A change of pace at least every seven to ten minutes can give participants the chance to refocus and renew their interest in the topic (Jones, Peters, & Shields, 2007). Thus, it is important that the pace of the teaching correspond to the attention span of the learners.

For teachers who are more comfortable with the lecture-only teaching style and learners who are more comfortable with passive learning, group involvement and active participation may seem problematic. Instructors may believe that they lose control of the class when they allow exercises to dominate classroom time. Learners may believe they would be learning more if they could get the information through lecture or readings. As teachers, we must remember that learners are capable of cognitively understanding a great deal of information, but that they can retain only segments, and will experience a value change based on only some of that learning experience. We can increase retention and behavior or value change by utilizing multiple training styles such as lecture, experiential activities, and small and large group activities, and by repeating the information throughout the session.

FACTORS AFFECTING LEARNING

Learning is not an automatic process. There are a number of factors that can inhibit the process. These may include one or more of the following:

- Learner believes he or she is at least as competent in the subject matter as the instructor.
- Learner resents authority figures such as the instructor.
- Learner is fearful of being seen as inferior or of being embarrassed.
- Learner is anxious.
- Learner has had a bad learning experience in the past.
- Learner comes to the session with other problems on his or her mind and is unable to focus.
- Learner is in class against his or her will and resents being there.
- Learner is interested in the material but is constrained by time and focused on other priorities.
- Learner has personal barriers or biases to learning about the topic. For example, a learner may be resistant to learning about a topic (e.g., evolution) that contradicts his or her religious beliefs.
- Learner has culturally based inhibitions to discussing or learning about the topic.
- Learner focuses on an annoying mannerism of the instructor.
- Learner is uncomfortable with the learning technique being used; this is common when learners are being introduced to technology for the first time.

Although it is difficult to address everyone's needs, it is important to meet as many needs as possible. To accomplish this goal, the instructor should assess learners' needs and issues. One way to do this is to simply ask the learners what their expectations are for the class session. There are more sophisticated assessment tools as well. Any of the ten methods described in part II can be used as a formative evaluation measure to make sure that a topic was understood before the class moves forward to the next topic. I prefer to use continuous evaluation mechanisms throughout the learning session to provide opportunities for learners to reflect on the content that was covered and to answer questions while information is fresh in the learners' minds. Sometimes learners have questions about issues that are beyond the scope of the instructor's responsibilities. In that case, you should acknowledge the value of the question, but politely tell the learner that the question is beyond the purview of the course. However, you may still be able to establish the value and relevance of the questions to the entire course.

PART II

Tools and Techniques

TOOLS

Ten Methods for Increasing Participation

Silberman (1996) identifies ten methods to encourage participation:

1. **Open discussions** are a great way to get learners involved but can become a nightmare if not managed properly. In order to make open discussions effective, it is important to put some thought into the expected outcome. Ask focused questions in order to guide the discussion and prevent long run-on discussions. You should also make sure that a few individuals do not monopolize the discussion. One way to prevent learners from simply restating what the text says is to begin by having one person restate what is in the text and then ask everyone else to apply the concept to a personal experience. You can use this method to stimulate discussion both in the classroom and in online courses. In web-based courses, you can post questions on a discussion board, and learners can respond to the thread.

2. **Response cards** are useful tools for stimulating interaction that allow learners to anonymously respond to questions. Distribute index cards at the beginning of a session, and have learners use them to answer questions. I have also had learners use them to share case examples to be discussed in class. You can collect and redistribute cards to small groups for discussion, or you can randomly select and read aloud cards for class discussion. The size of the index card is important, because it forces learners to give concise responses. (I usually like to use four-by-six cards.) You can use a variation of this technique for summative evaluation at the end of a session. Have learners use the cards to respond to a question that focuses on the key learning objective for that session in one minute. The one-minute time limit, like the size of the index cards, keeps the responses short and manageable. It also helps learners sharpen their critical-thinking and writing skills since it forces them to limit their response to a specific item. In large lectures, you can use response cards to encourage questions from the class. You can then sort them into categories and allow the class to respond to them.

3. **Polling** is a way to get learners to think about a topic. It can be used to gather data and stimulate discussion. A technique I use when I sense energy is low is a values voting technique. I ask everyone in the class to stand, and read a statement. If the learners agree with the statement, they raise their hands. If they strongly agree, they raise their hands and wave them. If they disagree with the statement, they put a thumb down; if they strongly disagree, they put their thumbs down and wave them. If they have no opinion, they cross their arms in front of them. This technique immediately engages the learners and allows them to express their opinions on value-laden issues. Polls can also be conducted with written surveys. The advantage to a written survey is that you can quantify the results and report them to the learners. For online courses, there is software available in the online course testing components that immediately tabulates responses to surveys completed online.

4. **Group discussions** allow for maximum interaction in discussion of a topic. This exercise is most helpful when you have sufficient time to process questions and issues. You can also use this technique for online courses. Learners can use the chat rooms in online course software to meet and to discuss questions posed by the instructor. As the instructor of the course, you can view a transcript of the chat session to see who participated without actually having to be there; however, you can also assure learners that you will not view discussions that take place in chat rooms so the learners know that discussions are confidential.

5. There are times, particularly in large lecture rooms with fixed seating, when it is difficult for learners to form small groups. Having students **pair up with learning partners** is a way to engage everyone, especially when there is not enough time for small group discussion. This group configuration facilitates the development of supportive relationships and is useful when learners are working on complex activities that do not lend themselves to large group configurations. Rather than asking if there are any questions, I often have learners turn to their neighbors and discuss key elements where there may be some confusion. Once learners have had a chance to discuss these elements, they are usually more comfortable formulating and sharing

their questions with the rest of the class. I find that this technique generates questions that are more thoughtful than when I simply ask, "Are there any questions?"

6. A technique you can use to make sure that everyone participates in a class is called **"a whip."** This is also a way to control learners' interactions to avoid everyone talking at the same time. To use a whip, pose a question or make a statement that you want the learners to respond to. Then begin with a learner at a particular place in the room and go around the room, allowing each learner to give a short response. Use whips when you want to obtain quick answers from each learner. You can begin a whip with a sentence stem such as, "One change I would make is. . . ." If a learner has nothing to say, you should allow him or her to pass.

7. There are a number of small group exercises that can stimulate the learning experience. One is the use of **panels**. Pose a question and then break the class into small groups to discuss the question. The small groups form panels to present their answers to the rest of the class. To expand the content, you can give different groups different topics or questions to discuss and present to the class. A variation on this is called "the jigsaw," where you give each group of learners material to learn and then divide the group up. You redistribute the learners so there is one person from each group in each new group. Within this newly reconfigured group, each person is responsible for teaching the material he or she learned in the original group to the rest of the group.

8. Another technique to encourage active learning is **"the fishbowl."** Here you divide the class into an inner discussion circle and an outer listening circle. You pose a question or topic and allow the members of the inner circle to discuss it while the members of the listening circle listen to the discussion. Have learners trade places so that everyone has a chance to participate in both circles. This technique is a good exercise to bring focus to large group discussions. This exercise can be time consuming, but is a good method for combining the virtues of large and small group discussion.

9. You can easily **modify game shows** such as *Jeopardy*, *Family Feud*, and *Who Wants to Be a Millionaire* for a fun classroom activity. Such

games are great tools to encourage participation and often appeal to the competitive nature of some learners. In addition, the game is a good summative evaluation technique to measure the learning outcomes of a particular session. There are even buzzer systems that you can purchase to enhance these activities in the classroom.

10. When learners ask questions, the focus is usually on the instructor or facilitator, not on the other learners in the group. However, learning takes place from all directions within the room. One way to promote classroom interaction and prevent top-down learning is to **have learners call on the next speaker**. The instructor selects one person to respond to a question or statement, and when that learner finishes speaking, he or she calls on the next speaker. This technique works well when there is a lot of interest in the discussion. In a variation on this technique, you can use a Nerf ball to designate the next speaker. A speaker throws the Nerf ball, and the person who catches it answers the question and then throws it to another learner. In an online class in a chat room, the person who responds to a question can call on another learner to answer the next question.*

Case Studies

What

Case studies can be a very effective way to involve learners and get them to apply what they are learning. They provide a description of a situation with enough detail to allow learners to analyze the issues and problems involved and decide on possible responses. Case studies are effective because they ground the information in real-life situations. Teachers can use case studies as preparation for a lecture. You can also use them as a formative evaluation to assess whether learners understand content. Case studies provide an opportunity for the learners to take a situation and apply a problem-solving technique to arrive at solutions. Seeing how the learners use a problem-solving process to arrive at solutions to the case will help you ascertain how the learners utilize critical-thinking techniques.

* From Silberman, M., *Active Learning: 101 Strategies to Teach Any Subject,* 1/e. Published by Allyn & Bacon, Boston, MA. Copyright by Pearson Education. Reprinted by permission of the publisher.

Why

You can use case studies to stimulate questions, to reinforce or explore the application of a specific concept, and to help learners pull together and summarize what they have learned. Sometimes teachers use case studies to convey content that they would otherwise need to cover in a lecture.

How to Create a Case Study

Developing an appropriate case is not difficult, but if not done carefully it can lead to great confusion. Here are steps you can follow as you create a clinically oriented case:

- Decide how you will use the case to help accomplish your teaching goals. There should be only one major learning point or goal for any case study, generally. Think about whether the case will require the learners to reason with basic concepts in order to deal successfully with the problems the case presents.
- Utilize your own experience as you develop a case. Instead of inventing a fictional case, rely on your experience with the subject matter in developing the case study. This approach infuses the case with a sense of realism to which learners can relate, and it conveys your expertise on the topic.
- Write a brief case with a minimum of extraneous information. The goal is to generate interest in and discussion on a specific concept. The more information you provide, the more likely learners are to focus on the nonessential information. In addition, what often happens when too many variables are added to a case study is that learners debate approaches or methods that are unrelated to the intended goal.
- Once you have written your case, ask peers to review the case with an eye on the key teaching point.
- Think about the time frame in which the case will fit. If the case is too complicated or introduced prematurely, then the learners may lose interest in it and become frustrated. Learners need time to think about, digest, and ponder the case. It is better to have too much time than too little when considering a case.

24

I Decide how the case fits in with the content of the lecture. Does it augment the presentation? Will it enhance small group discussion focusing on relevant material? Does it introduce problem-solving behavior that will allow the learners to think critically through a situation? Will learners be forced to integrate material from a variety of disciplines and use higher-order thinking skills?

I Choose a format that will allow for the most flexibility in terms of the desired outcomes.

I Decide what resources or instructional materials are needed to enhance the case presentation. Would inviting an expert consultant or a guest lecturer to class enhance the discussion about the case? Make sure you have instructional resources like flipcharts and markers.

I Decide whether prompting questions should be a formal part of the case. Identify the critical questions that learners should discuss.

I Decide how you are going to evaluate the success of the case study design. Did the design achieve what you had hoped? (Kaufman, Mennin, & Waterman, 1989)

Debriefing the Activity

Make sure you leave enough time to debrief the case so that learners can think about how they would apply what they learned from the case to their own environment (this is affective learning). Here are some debriefing tips:

I Depending on the time available, have individual learners or a few or all of the small groups report on the outcomes of their work.

I Encourage feedback and questions from the class.

I Provide feedback, if it is appropriate.

I Summarize the key learning points of the discussion and any open issues or questions.

I Record these key points on a flipchart and post it in the room.

I Explain how this activity links to the purpose of the session.

Role-Play Activities

What

Role-playing enables learners to practice a particular skill in a safe simulated environment. Role-plays are often conducted in small groups of three. This allows one person (the practitioner) to practice, one person (the client/patient) to interact with the practitioner, and one person (the observer) to provide feedback. Roles can be rotated to allow each person the opportunity to practice, if time allows.

Why

Role-playing is the closest simulation to the actual application of skills that can be achieved in a classroom setting. It involves the learners in practicing a skill and gives them immediate feedback.

How to Prepare for Role-Play Activities

You can use these tips to prepare for role-play activities:

- Before the class breaks into groups, review the goals and instructions for the activity and clearly identify the roles players will assume for the activity.
- Prepare instructions for the activity on a flipchart in advance to ensure that all key points are covered.
- Determine the time limit for the activity.
- Determine how to divide the class for the activity; everyone should have a role.
- Determine how to monitor and debrief the activity.

Debriefing the Activity

Debrief in small groups. Start with reactions from the practitioner, followed by the client/patient, then the observer. Each person should discuss

- General reactions regarding how he or she felt in the role,
- What he or she thinks went well,
- What he or she would do differently, and
- Specific behaviors that worked or did not seem to work.

Debrief with the entire class.

I Ask each group to comment on one key lesson learned, and record these on a flipchart so all learners can see the other groups' responses.
I Encourage feedback and questions from the groups.
I Explain how this activity relates to the purpose of the session.

VISUAL AIDS

In addition to mastering various instructional methods, teachers should become comfortable and proficient in using various visual aids.

Video

What

A short trigger tape or video at the beginning of a session or when you introduce a new topic can stimulate interest in the topic, identify important issues, and establish the relevance of the subject matter. It also provides a common reference point for all the learners. The tape should generally be only a few minutes in length. There are a number of resources, such as YouTube or Hulu, where you can gain access to short videos with minimal costs.

Why

Trigger tapes or videos provide a good vehicle for active learning because teachers can use them to identify key issues and stimulate discussion. Do not miss the opportunity to structure some type of activity or discussion around the trigger tape for each module, even if it is very brief.

How to Use Videos

In preparation, you should do the following:

I Check the equipment in advance to ensure that it is functioning properly and the tape is not damaged.
I Adjust the position of the screen for good visibility and make sure the volume is appropriate.

I Make sure the videotape is inserted and set to the beginning of the segment to be shown.

I Find out how to get help if there are any technical difficulties.

I View the tape in advance and make notes on key points to bring up in the discussion.

During the module, you should do the following:

I Briefly introduce the tape and explain why you are showing it.

I Help learners focus on the right points by providing direction on what they should look for.

I Suggest to learners that they may want to take some notes as they watch the video.

I Show the video.

I Use your prepared questions as a guide to facilitate a discussion.

I Summarize the key points of the discussion and link this activity to the next part of the session.

If time permits, you can add these activities:

I Ask the learners to discuss one or two questions in pairs or groups of three and then briefly report a few key points from their discussion to the whole group.

I Ask one or two people to share their own experiences in situations similar to that shown in the trigger video.

I Use guiding questions to elicit what they would do in order to obtain a different result.

I Ask the group, "Based on what you have seen, what questions would you like to have answered?"

Here are some important reminders:

I Keep the discussions focused and adhere to the time limits you have set.

I Have reasonable expectations regarding what it will and will not be possible to cover in the allotted time.

I Explain how learners can get more information if they are interested.

Debriefing the Activity

Although debriefing as a whole group is possible, to maximize the discussion it is best to have the learners debrief in small groups. The video was introduced to support or enhance a particular content area that could be taught more effectively through visual means. Although all learners viewed the same video, their perception of the content is based on each individual's value orientation. Therefore, it is important to

I Ask for reactions about the video that relate to the individual's feelings on how the content related to the subject matter at hand;

I Ask learners to discuss what additional questions the video triggered; and

I Be prepared to provide additional resources for the learners to obtain further information on the topic.

Flipcharts

Flipcharts are good tools for recording key learning points from discussion, questions that need to be answered, and instructions for activities. They provide visual variety and help create an active learning environment. Some tips for using flipcharts follow:

I Make the lettering about two inches high to ensure that those in the back of the room can read the flipcharts.

I Use a variety of colors. It is visually pleasing and effective to alternate colors from line to line when you are listing items on a flipchart.

I Label each flipchart page with a title (e.g., "Objectives," "Questions").

I Make sure that a roll of masking tape is available so that you can place pages on the wall for future reference. It helps to prepare pieces of tape in advance.

I Keep it simple. Use key words rather than whole sentences.

I Use the learners' own words whenever possible rather than paraphrasing. This encourages the learners to be actively involved in the process.

I If you do not have a cofacilitator, consider having one of the learners act as scribe to record key points during the discussion. Be prepared to assist the scribe as needed to ensure that he or she records key points accurately.

I For activities like the trigger tapes or case studies, use the plus/minus technique to structure ideas about what went well and what could have been done differently: Draw a line down the middle of a flipchart and label one column with a plus and one column with a minus. First, ask learners to list the positive points or the things that went well. Record these on the plus side. Next, ask learners to list the things they would change or do differently the next time. Record these on the minus side. Determine which ideas for change the class should implement.

ROOM SET-UP

The way that a room is set up is a statement that you are making to your learners about the learning experience. If the room is set up in a traditional classroom mode, then the focus is at the front of the room, on you as the instructor (the sage on the stage). If you arrange the seating in a U or circle, then the expectation is that everyone will interact. There are some rooms, like large lecture halls, where it is impossible to change the set-up, but even in these rooms, you can use activities like small group discussion to promote active learning. A U-shaped set-up maximizes the interactions between learners and between learners and the instructor. It also facilitates eye contact. In the U-shaped set-up, there are no learners in the back row. The teacher is free to walk around inside the U, and for each learner to be in the front row.

TRAINING METHODS

Lecture

What

The lecture method is a standard technique for delivering information. When the content is relevant to the needs of the learner and when the speaker is motivating and interesting, the lecture format can be an effective learning modality.

Why

The lecture method is efficient when a teacher needs to quickly impart large amount of information. It is also a way for the instructor to reach many learners at one time.

Potential Problems

There are some inherent problems with the lecture method, particularly if it is conducted over an extended period. These problems include the following:

I Lecture is a passive form of learning designed to impart information. As we know from the study of adult learning, adults learn best when they can apply new information and skills to solve an immediate problem or need (Knowles, 1980). If the goal is for learners to learn new skills, then teachers must use new techniques.

I Lecture appeals primarily to learners who prefer auditory modalities. Teachers can use visual aids to appeal to visual learners.

I Lecture assumes that all learners need the same information delivered at the same time and at the same pace.

I During a lecture, the learner's attention span tends to decrease with each passing minute. Karl Smith, a master trainer, recommends stopping at least every eight minutes during a lecture to involve the learners in a discussion or activity in order to add variety and stimulate learners (D. Johnson, R. Johnson, & Smith, 1998).

Enhancing Lectures to Make Them Active Learning Experiences

Lectures by nature lead to passive learning. There are ways to increase the effectiveness of lectures by combining them with techniques that encourage involvement and participation. It takes some careful planning, but here are some suggestions for making the learning that occurs during lectures more active:

- Plan to grab the attention of the audience in the first few seconds of the lecture. You can do this by using a whip technique or having learners partner up to get everyone talking at the beginning of the session.
- Show a trigger tape to stimulate group discussion. This is a good way to provide everyone with a common reference point to encourage discussion and group problem solving.
- Have learners discuss why the subject matter is important. You may want to introduce this discussion with a case example or personal story.
- Provide an overview of your objectives and involve learners in determining the focus of the learning.
- Provide opportunities for learners to record and reflect on their own thoughts and questions on a specific topic. Use polls or response cards to engage the learners in the development of thoughts and questions.
- Use visuals such as slides, videos, flipcharts, and handouts.
- Stop periodically so the learners can discuss key points or so you can engage them in an activity that will help them reflect on or see how to apply what they are learning.
- Provide opportunities for learners to share their experience with each other. This can be done as a class or in small groups or pairs.
- Involve the learners in actively summarizing the key points of the lecture. You can do this by asking learners to reflect on the lessons they have learned so far or having them apply the key points to a case study.

I Tell them what you are going to teach, teach it to them, and then tell them what you taught them.

Debriefing the Activity

As previously mentioned, adult attention spans are between seven and fifteen minutes. Therefore, it is important to assess whether the lecture truly met the expectations that it was intended to address. There are a number of ways to assess whether the content was understood by the learners. Some of these may be classified as CAT (classroom assessment techniques):

I Ask the learners to write a minute paper highlighting the key points that were covered in the lecture.

I Ask targeted questions about the content to see if it was understood and have the learners provide either oral or written responses.

I A quiz or the use of clickers in the classroom can also measure knowledge. With a clicker system, a multiple-choice quiz using PowerPoint can be created; the learners respond using the clicker system.

These methods provide feedback for the teacher as to whether the content was understood at the time of delivery. They are not individual learner assessments but rather information for the teacher.

PowerPoint

What

PowerPoint and other presentation software packages can enhance your lecture by helping you organize material and present it in a visually stimulating format.

Why

PowerPoint is one way to visually improve a lecture and appeal to visual learners. It integrates visual techniques and stimuli with the auditory style of lecture. Copies of the PowerPoint slides also make easy handouts.

Potential Problems

PowerPoint can certainly enhance the lecture method, but there are some inherent problems with it if it is used over an extended period. These problems include the following:

I PowerPoint, like lecture, is a passive form of learning designed to impart information. The presenter can become so involved with the PowerPoint slides that he or she stops focusing on the learners.

I PowerPoint is presented in a linear fashion. Once you begin a PowerPoint presentation, you are enslaved to the order and content of the slides. This may not conform to the needs of the learners or the order in which they want to learn the information.

I Depending on the power of the LCD projector you use, you may need to dim the lights. This can present problems for learners who are tired and more likely to tune out in a dimly lit room.

Tips for Using PowerPoint

Here are some PowerPoint tips:

I For better readability, each slide should follow the rule of 6-6-24: six lines per slide, six words to a line, and no text smaller than twenty-four-point font.

I Enhance the discussion environment during your presentation by striking the *B* key on the keyboard to darken the screen. Striking *B* again brings the presentation back. Striking the *W* key makes the screen turn white.

I Less is more. Some people put full sentences or even paragraphs on a PowerPoint slide. This can be problematic since people have trouble reading too much on one slide, and an overwhelming amount of text makes the slide look busy, which can be frustrating to the people reading the slide. Keep it simple with plenty of white space on the slide.

❙ Learn to use the software's commands and functions (found under the action setting tab) to hyperlink to websites or other files or slides. You do not have to exit PowerPoint to show another program or a webpage—just plan ahead and make sure you have inputted the links before the session begins.

Debriefing the Activity

Many of the same debriefing techniques for lectures can be used for PowerPoint, since most teachers these days use PowerPoint to enhance the lecture. There are other techniques that can also be used to debrief PowerPoint, one of which is to turn the PowerPoint into a game format. There are a number of templates available to assist in creating game shows, such as *Jeopardy*, in a PowerPoint format.

ACTIVE DISCUSSION TOOLS AND TECHNIQUES

Facilitating Discussions

What

Teachers often use the group discussion technique along with lecture to provide variety and give learners a chance to reflect on what they are learning. When the entire class participates in group discussions, the instructor normally facilitates discussion. The instructor may also ask a learner to help record key points made during the discussion. A variation of the discussion technique is to divide the class into groups of three to five people and provide them with one or more topics to discuss. Each group should then elect a spokesperson to report the findings back to the class. It is important to assign roles to each member of the group. These can include a **leader** (the person responsible for controlling the group interactions), **recorder** (who records the decisions of the group), **reporter** (who reports the results to the class), and **process reporter** (who records the process or the steps that the group followed to accomplish the task).

Why

Adult learners have a need to share their own experiences, hear the experiences of others, and relate those experiences to what they are learning. It is important not to have too much discussion since you need time to present new content. However, discussion is a good way to assess whether the content that you presented was understood.

How to Prepare for Large Group Discussions

These are steps you should take to prepare for the discussion:

- Identify the goals and the key points to be covered.
- Make a list of open-ended questions that will elicit the key points.
- Decide on the time frame for the activity.

What to Do During the Activity

Here are some tips for conducting successful and fruitful group discussions:

- Explain the purpose of the activity.
- Ask open-ended questions.
- Allow time for learners to respond.
- Encourage participation by linking comments and calling on individuals for their opinions.
- Stay flexible, and do not force a desired point if it is not offered. You can make the point at the end of the session if a learner does not offer it.
- Provide positive reinforcement for learners' comments.
- Respond to questions.
- Periodically review and tie the discussion back to the key learning points.
- Summarize the conversation and record key points on a flipchart, or ask someone else to do so.

Debriefing the Activity

Discussions can easily move off the key point or purpose for the activity. Therefore, it is important to keep focused on the intent of the activity. Teachers can achieve this during small group discussions within the larger group by wandering around the room to make sure that each small group is staying on topic. For the larger group discussions, it is important for the teacher not to be sidetracked. Once the activity is completed, it is important to solicit feedback, either orally or in writing, as to how the discussion helped to support the content presented. Short reflection papers are tools that teachers can use to assess the effectiveness of the discussion.

Online Instruction or Hybrid Models

What

More and more programs are looking to electronic media to provide instructions. Some of these are solely online whereas others use a combination of online and face-to-face programs, called hybrid. One of the benefits of online or hybrid instruction is that it allows the learner to gather the material asynchronously, or in his or her own time, and not have to be in a classroom to learn. This provides opportunities for learners to learn on their own schedule and not rely on the structure of being in a face-to-face classroom. One of the downsides is that the learner expects the instructor to be accessible during the same time, and so there is an expectation that the instructor can be engaged at all hours of the day, every day of the week. As a result, the instructor must create some limits in responding to learners.

Whereas many institutions see online instruction as a tool to be able to electronically create large classrooms without having to be concerned about the bricks and mortar of traditional classrooms, and whereas learners like the idea of being able to take a class in the comfort of their homes, the development of online instruction continues to adhere to adult learning principles. In fact, online or hybrid instruction relies more heavily on the adult learning principles than it does in an in-person or face-to-face class. Palloff and Pratt (2011) identify ten points that define the excellent online instructor:

1. The instructor understands the differences between face-to-face and online teaching in developing and implementing the online class.
2. The instructor is committed to online instruction and uses it to his or her advantage.

3. The instructor is able to establish a presence early in the course and encourages the students to do the same.

4. The instructor is highly motivated and is able to motivate the students.

5. The instructor understands the importance of community building and devotes time to it at the beginning of the class.

6. The instructor promotes interactivity between students by offering good discussion questions.

7. The instructor incorporates collaborative work into the course design and delivery of content online.

8. The instructor respects students as partners in the learning process.

9. The instructor is active and engaged throughout the course, providing timely feedback.

10. The instructor is open, flexible, compassionate, and responsive, and leads by example (Palloff & Pratt, 2011, 13–14).

Thus, online instruction is not as easy as posting lectures, but rather involves a different thinking process and a different way of engaging the learners. Not everyone can jump into online instruction because it involves a willingness to experiment with technology. In addition, all participants need to be comfortable enough to make mistakes. The online instructor should have a presence by frequently being involved in the online environment. This will involve being open, flexible, fair, and honest. The online instructor needs to be organized and must have good time-management skills.

In creating an online or hybrid course, it is important that the teacher not take on more than he or she can handle. Some teachers perceive that seat count for an online course should be limited; however, many times institutions believe they can maximize the class size since it is an online format and they are not restricted by physical bricks-and-mortar classroom sizes. Within the online course, it can be difficult to manage too many learners, and a large group can impede interactions. Therefore, try to keep the class between twenty to twenty-five learners. In addition, the role of the instructor is different in the online class. As previously mentioned, the learners expect the instructor to be accessible at all hours of the day, every day of the week. It is important to set limits and identify days and times that you will or will not be available. Finally, it is important to make sure you have both technical and developmental supports to think through the content and the formatting of how you will develop the course. Some of these may be predesigned through learning management systems (LMS) that the institution subscribes to, whereas others are open-source and involve more design and development by either the instructor or the institution. Remember the KIS principle and "keep it simple," because the more complicated it becomes for the learners, the less likely it is that they will access the site and use what you are providing. Also, remember the ten-second rule: if someone cannot find something on a webpage in less than ten seconds, then he or she will move to another site. The learners need to be able to find your content within ten seconds or they will not access it.

Online Discussion

A key component to online or hybrid education is the online discussion. Online discussions allow a group of learners to collectively inquire into and explore a topic while they work online—for example, on the web, in a web-enhanced course, or through an electronic mailing list (list serve). This gives learners an opportunity to perform higher-order thinking, such as analysis, synthesis, evaluation, reflective thinking, and problem solving. The process is collaborative, transforming, and democratic. The facilitator of the online discussion has a particularly important role, which includes acting as a role model. Therefore, it is especially important for the facilitator to show enthusiasm for the medium as well as the process. Furthermore, the facilitator needs to demonstrate confidence that the learners will be contributing to each other's learning. This is critical since the role of the facilitator is to facilitate and help learners learn, and not to dominate the discussion.

Why

As programs reach out to learners and it becomes more difficult to get everyone in the same place at the same time, educators are using different methods to enhance the learning process. These include computer-assisted techniques, such as electronic mailing lists (list serves), chat groups, and web courses, which bring together people who are geographically distant.

Teachers can use tools like Skype or Google+ Hangout to connect groups of people together synchronously even though they might be miles apart. The procedures for online discussions are the same as those for regular discussions, but the online medium does create different challenges.

TECHNIQUES TO ENCOURAGE GOOD DISCUSSION

The facilitator can employ a number of techniques to encourage and sustain good discussions. These include the following:

I Paraphrasing
I Checking for understanding and asking for clarification
I Complimenting learners for responding
I Using examples or alternative perspectives to seek elaboration
I Using humor or prodding to encourage additional contributions
I Seeking agreement on summary themes or issues
I Mediating differences of opinion (Silberman, 1996)

Questioning Techniques

Skillful questioning is the key to effective facilitation. This involves using open-ended questions tailored to the online environment and the requirements of the discussion. Key questions need to provide some structure and direction to the discussion. Questions need to be phrased clearly, logically, and specifically at the learners' level of experience. Depending on the objective, teachers can tailor questions so the learners must use different types of thinking (e.g., synthesis or analysis).

As a facilitator, try to avoid answering your own questions. Questions should stimulate thinking and ideas from the group. This means that you need to be comfortable asking open-ended questions and allowing enough time for people to respond, asking questions of specific individuals, redirecting a question to the learner, and relaying a question to another participant or to the class. A technique I use is to count to ten after asking a question to allow time for the learners to think and understand the meaning of the question. Waiting through a count to ten also means that you are encouraging the learners to respond. After counting to ten, if no one has answered the question, then it may be helpful for you to reframe the question and ask it again.

Open-Ended and General Questions

These are questions that you can throw out to the whole class. It may be useful to ask the same question more than once to get different answers. Use these questions when you wish to give everyone a chance to respond. Note that these questions work best if learners cannot answer them with "yes" or "no."

Questions Directed to Specific Individuals

Call on a person for specific information that he or she has, or to involve someone who is not participating. Always begin the question by stating the person's name so the learner knows he or she is the one you expect to respond.

Redirecting a Question to the Learner

A learner may ask you a question to get your opinion. At this point, you need to decide if you will answer the question, redirect it, or both answer and redirect. Redirecting a question back to the learner is a way for you to avoid giving an opinion or answer, to encourage the learner to think for himself or herself, and to get others' opinions.

Relaying a Question to Another Participant or to the Class

An excellent way to get more people involved in the discussion is to use relay questions. Introduce a relay question by asking a learner to redirect his or her question to another learner or to the class as a whole. This allows you to avoid giving an opinion or answer and gets others involved. When it is appropriate, it allows you to call on someone you know has experience or knowledge related to the subject matter.

Specific Uses and Examples of Questions

You might draw on some of these questions to facilitate a discussion that maximizes learner participation.

To get the discussion started, ask

- "What are the main purposes of . . . ?"
- "What is your understanding of . . . ?"
- "In your opinion, Tyrone, what effects might that have on . . . ?"

To capture and maintain interest, ask convergent questions or closed questions such as

- "Of all the . . . , which seems to be the most appropriate and why?"
- "You identified . . . as the critical point. What does that mean to you?"

To keep group discussion going, and to encourage learners to contribute more information and ideas, ask divergent or open-ended questions such as

- "That is an interesting point. How do the rest of you feel about that?"
- "What other ideas or thoughts do you have on the issue?"
- "Given the pros we just discussed, what would be some of the cons concerning . . . ?"

To get nonparticipating learners involved, ask

- "Given your background working with . . . , Kate, how do you see this affecting the individuals with whom you work?"
- "Jung, how have you dealt with this type of situation in the past?"
- "Rachel, could you share your perspective on the issue?"

To clarify information or comments, ask

- "Could you share an example of your point of view?"
- "How does this solution compare with what has been attempted in the past?"
- "Kira, how would you paraphrase Jacob's point?"

To keep discussion focused, ask

▌ "Excellent idea. How does that address the question?"
▌ "This has been an interesting discussion; however, getting back to the initial question, how does this relate to . . . ?"

To move the discussion on to the next topic or create a transition, ask

▌ "Given the ideas presented, what would be the next logical step?"
▌ "Now that the causes of . . . have been addressed, how could we best address the issue?"
▌ "Your thoughts help to explain . . . , but how does this relate to . . . ?"

To assess and evaluate the information, ask

▌ "Do the facts justify the conclusions? Why or why not?"
▌ "How does this compare with your experience?"
▌ "Given the information, what conclusions can be drawn?"

To handle problem learners, ask

▌ "Greg, do you generally view matters from a . . . perspective?"
▌ "It appears that we have two very different points of view. Could we discuss this some other time?"
▌ "It is perfectly fine to have differing views; it helps us understand the issue from different perspectives. Now, let's move on to. . . ."

To suggest desired responses, ask

▌ "What is the most efficient way to find a solution to . . . ?"
▌ "What steps would you take to get to . . . ?"

To determine learners' understanding or to get feedback, ask

▌ "Can you identify the steps that make the process work?"
▌ "Can you give an example of when this step did not work?"
▌ "If you were working with . . . , how would you apply the steps?"

To get agreement on a solution or to reach a conclusion, ask

▎ "What can you conclude from the discussion of . . . ?"
▎ "Does anyone disagree with what has been said? If so, please help us understand your perspective and reasoning."
▎ "When you look at this . . . , what does it mean for . . . ?"

Answering Questions

In general, the facilitator should facilitate, not participate. If you, as a facilitator, participate too much in the discussion, you are setting yourself up as an expert. This will generally have a negative effect on the participation of the learners. You should give careful thought to how and why you are answering a specific question and use your best judgment based on the situation. Types of questions that teachers should answer include

▎ Requests for clarification of the goals of the activity,
▎ Requests for clarification of the question, and
▎ Requests for factual information as it relates to the topic that the learner may have missed when it was presented.

Acknowledging Participation

The way a facilitator responds to learners in a discussion affects how fully learners participate. Your goals as you respond to comments should be to remain open to a variety of ideas, to thank learners for their participation, to avoid revealing your personal positive or negative feelings about a particular comment, and to be respectful of all contributions.

Remaining neutral and respectful encourages positive participation from everyone. In acknowledging responses, there are a number of tactics facilitators can use:

▎ React neutrally. Do this to convey interest and to keep the person talking. Say something like, "I see," or "That's interesting. Tell me more."

I Explore. Do this to gather more information and help learners explore all sides of an issue. Say something like, "What do you think the most important problem is that we need to deal .with?"

I Restate. Do this to show you are listening and to encourage more participation. Say something like, "If I understand you correctly, your idea is . . . ," or "So that experience was quite powerful for you. Am I correct?"

I Summarize. Do this to pull together different ideas and to reemphasize key points of the conversation. Say something like, "So far we have heard three different ideas about how to handle that problem. They are. . . ."

I Provide input. Do this if you believe you have an important point to make that is not coming out in the discussion. Be careful not to provide too much input, or you will discourage participation. Always try asking open-ended questions to elicit the point before you make the point yourself.

BE PREPARED FOR DIFFICULT PARTICIPANTS

Learners come in many different forms. Ideally, they would all come to class motivated and invested in the learning process. Unfortunately, every class will most likely have at least one difficult learner.

For those occasional difficult learners, here is a step-by-step approach that usually works:

I Make eye contact.
I Move toward him or her, and stand close by.
I Involve him or her in the activity.
I Use humor to subtly encourage the learner to stop what he or she is doing.

If these steps do not work, talk to the individual outside class. Your last resort: ask the offender to leave!

You can discuss difficult learners by asking your learners to identify characteristics of each type of difficult classmate:

I The know-it-all
I The naysayer
I The monopolizer
I The chatterbox
I The reluctant learner
I The preacher
I The unresponsive learner

The Know-It-All

The know-it-all thinks he or she is an expert in everything being covered. This learner wants everyone to know how much he or she knows. Avoid debate with this person. Teachers never win; instead, debate leads to a power struggle for control of the class. Acknowledge his or her expertise and ask if this learner minds being called on for support on various issues as the class proceeds. This usually defuses the situation and gives this type of learner the attention he or she is seeking.

The Naysayer

The naysayer refuses to see how what is being covered can or will work and is bent on exploring why it will not work. There are a number of reasons why a learner may be a naysayer. If you do not handle this learner appropriately, you may find yourself spending the bulk of your time countering negative comments. As with the know-if-all, if the instructor debates the naysayer, other learners may feel left out. In addition, it is very difficult not to become defensive with such learners. As a rule of thumb, if a naysayer is in the audience, you can stop him or her with a comment like, "I see you have some problems with what I am saying. I appreciate what you are saying, but there are people here who want to see how this will work." If the naysayer continues to contradict you, consider pulling the person aside during a break and asking him or her to leave since he or she seems unwilling to try to work with the group.

The Monopolizer

A monopolizer may attempt to spend a great deal of time reinforcing what is being said or contradicting the content. The monopolizer may simply have a lot of questions or a lot of stories or relevant information. This type of learner can become very annoying to others. Teachers walk a fine line in attempting to limit the participation of this type of learner. Monopolizers are rarely hostile. Instead, they seem to thrive on the attention. Some teachers recommend bluntly saying, "We have heard a lot of good information from you today. Let's now give others a chance to speak." Depending on the setting, other learners might welcome this approach. However, it may make other learners feel afraid to participate because they are afraid the teacher will suggest that they are speaking too much. A more gentle approach to use with a monopolizer is simply to avoid eye contact or, if possible, walk to another part of the room while you are speaking. Obviously, choosing which approach to use is your call.

The Chatterbox

The chatterbox seems to have forgotten that a class is taking place. He or she carries on conversations with others during class, seemingly oblivious to how distracting and rude such behavior is. Although it may be uncomfortable to put a halt to the chatterbox's behavior, this chatter is most likely disruptive to other learners. To intervene, simply point out to this person that the conversation is distracting. A more subtle approach is to continue teaching while you walk over and stand by the learner. Few people will continue a sideline conversation in this situation. If they do, it is appropriate to call them on it.

The Reluctant Learner

The reluctant learner may have brought work from the office or may be reading a magazine or newspaper during the class. Although this may seem less disruptive than some other difficult types, this learner's actions are conveying a negative message to other learners. The message is, "Although I may have to be here, this class isn't important enough to deserve my full attention." The teacher should not take this behavior personally, but should not ignore this behavior, either. You deserve respect for the preparation and the work you have put into the session. Ask the reluctant learner to put the newspaper or magazine away. You may do this in a joking manner; for example, you might say, "Wow, it's hard to believe there's any news half as interesting as what I'm saying. Do you suppose it could wait until a break or until our session is over?" Also, if this learner is doing work from the office, acknowledge how busy he or she must be, but ask for the learner's attention because the knowledge you are imparting is sure to help in his or her work.

The Preacher

The preacher learner has values. Of course, other learners have values, too, but the preacher learner frequently vocalizes his or her values during the class. These values are most frequently expressed when the subject matter conflicts with the learner's beliefs (e.g., sex, condom distribution, drug use). Never debate or attempt to modify this person's values. Values take years to develop and will not change in a five-minute, two-hour, or six-hour debate. Acknowledge the learner's values (without editorializing) and move on. If he or she is persistent, acknowledge him or her and point out that not everyone shares his or her values. You can defuse the situation by stating to the entire group that it is important to recognize that not everyone shares the same set of values, but that everyone should respect each other's values.

The Unresponsive Learner

Unresponsive learners can be considered difficult learners only because they are very difficult for the teacher to read. These individuals tend not to take an active role in brainstorming, asking questions, or other exercises. An unresponsive learner's body language is often very difficult to read and offers the teacher little feedback. These learners may be totally enthralled with the teaching or may be daydreaming. They also may maintain this stance to avoid being called on or challenged by an exercise. The only way to know is to check in with this type of learner. For instance, during a brainstorming exercise, instead of starting with a request for people to volunteer input, ask an unresponsive learner what he or she thinks. The learner's reaction should give sufficient information regarding the reasons for his or her behavior. Some unresponsive learners simply need a little encouragement or ego stroking to become active learners.

Dealing with Difficult Learners

Ask your learners if they can think of any other types of difficult classmates that everyone should know about. Brainstorm ways to handle these people. Point out that a classroom session should never become focused on the difficult person. The teacher must always remain in control of the classroom. Instructors should learn to use the difficult learner to their benefit. As you become accustomed to working with the material, it will become apparent how to do this.

YOUR PERSONAL STYLE

Every teacher develops his or her own personal style. It is important to express your individual style and not mimic someone else's. A few points to keep in mind are the following:

I Find a happy medium between pacing around the room and standing still in front of the group.

I Use gestures to emphasize points. Gestures should be natural and purposeful.

I Speak to the learners, not to the slides or walls. Eye contact is imperative.

I Vary the volume and tone of your voice to avoid sounding monotonous.

I Be conscious of the speed of your delivery. Some variation in speed is good, but avoid talking too slowly (which can be boring) or too fast (which can be annoying).

I Make an effort to project your voice to the most distant part of the room. Use a microphone if necessary.

I Enunciate clearly. Pronounce words correctly.

I Dress professionally; err on the side of being too formal.

I If you have pockets, let them act as a fashion statement, and keep your hands out of them.

I Avoid unnecessary distractions like rattling pocket change or wearing too much jewelry.

CONCLUSION

Making the learning experience memorable yet informative is a challenge for all of us. This guide provides some basic hints and tools that you can integrate into your own teaching style. You should use the ones that work for you to create a more active learning experience for learners.

It is important to remember to use assessment and evaluative tools throughout the session. Sometimes the teacher asks at the end of a session if there are any questions and gets silence. Does this mean that there were no questions? It tends to be more of a statement of how comfortable the learners were asking questions throughout the session and how uncomfortable they are asking question in an overly controlled environment. Now that you are familiar with these activities and debriefing techniques, you can create an open environment in which learners freely and openly ask questions. I also find that conducting a formative assessment throughout the session leads to more dialogue, which gives me a good understanding of whether the learners understand the content.

I try to end each session with three questions: "What was most helpful?" "What was least helpful?" and "What would you have liked to see me do differently?" I realize that by asking these questions I am opening myself up to criticism; however, I am truly open to feedback, and I prefer to give learners an opportunity to provide that feedback orally as well as through written assessments and immediately. I have found that this creates a more trusting environment and makes the learners feel more invested in the learning process. Creating a supportive and open environment does a lot to enhance the learning experience.

RECOMMENDED READINGS

Anderson, L. W., & Krathwohl, D. R. (Eds.). (2001). *A taxonomy for learning, teaching, and assessing.* New York: Longman.

Angelo, T. (1993). A teacher's dozen: Fourteen general, research-based principles for improving higher learning in our classrooms. *AAHE Bulletin, 45*(8), 3–7.

Bevis, E. M., & Watson, J. (1989). *Toward a caring curriculum: A new pedagogy for nursing.* New York: National League for Nursing.

Brookfield, S. (1994). *Teaching and learning in the college classroom.* Needham Heights, MA: Ginn Press.

Buchanan, E. A. (2000). Going the extra mile: Serving distance education students with resources and services. *Syllabus, 13*(3), 44–47.

Dyche, J. (1982). *Educational program development for employees in health-care agencies.* Calabasas, CA: Tri-Oak Educational Division.

Education for Physicians on End-of-Life Care. (1999). *EPEC project.* Chicago: Robert Wood Johnson Foundation.

Elderedge, J. D. (1993). A problem-based learning curriculum in transition: The emerging role of the library. *Bulletin of the Medical Library Association, 81*(3), 310–315.

Everhart, R. L. (2000). Enterprise systems and distance learning: Creating services for connected learners. *Syllabus, 13*(9), 48–51.

Friedman, B. D., & Neuman, K. M. (2001). Learning plans: A tool for forging allegiances in social work education. *Teaching in Social Work, 21*(3/4), 123–138.

Grasha, A. F. (1996). *Teaching with style.* Pittsburgh, PA: Alliance.

Hawkins, R. L. (1994). Teaching teachers how to teach with technology: Do's and don'ts. *Computing Teacher, 12*(8), 16–17.

Krathwohl, D. R., Bloom, B. S., & Masia, B. B. (1973). *Taxonomy of educational objectives. Handbook II: Affective domain.* New York: David McKay.

Martinez, M. (1999). Using learning orientation to investigate how individuals learn successfully on the Web. *Technical Communication, 46*(4), 470–487.

McKeachie, W. J., Chism, N., Menges, R., Svinicki, M., & Weinstein, C. E. (1994). *Teaching tips: Strategies and theory for college and university teachers.* Lexington, MA: D. C. Heath.

Quirk, M. E. (1994). *How to learn and teach in medical school: A learner centered approach.* Springfield, MA: Charles C Thomas.

Schwenk, T., & Whitman, N. (1987). *The physician as teacher.* Baltimore: Williams & Wilkins.

Silberman, M. (1990). *Active training: A handbook of techniques, designs, case examples, and tips.* New York: Lexington Books.

Silberman, M. (1996). *Active learning: 101 strategies to teach any subject.* Needham Heights, MA: Allyn & Bacon.

Silberman, M. (2006). *Teaching actively: Eight steps and 32 strategies to spark learning in any classroom.* Boston: Allyn & Bacon.

Whitman, N. (1990). *Creative medical teaching.* Salt Lake City: University of Utah School of Medicine.

REFERENCES

Allen, K. N., & Friedman, B. D. (2010). Affective learning: A taxonomy for teaching social work values. *Journal of Social Work Values and Ethics, 7*(2).

Barrett, D. (2012). How "flipping" the classroom can improve the traditional lecture. *Chronicle of Higher Education* (February 24), A16–A18.

Biggs, J., & Tang, C. (2011). *Teaching for quality learning at university: What the student does.* London: McGraw Hill.

Bloom, B. S. (Ed.). (1956). *Taxonomy of educational objectives: The classification of educational goals.* New York: Longmans, Green.

Friedman, B. D., Ward, D., & Biagianti, A. (1998). Using technology to forge new allegiances in social work education. *New Technology in Human Services, 11*(2), 13–18.

Johnson, D. W., Johnson, R. T., & Smith, K. A. (1998). *Active learning: Cooperation in the college classroom.* Edina, MN: Interaction Book Company.

Johnstone, A. H., & Percival, F. (1976). Attention breaks in lectures. *Education in Chemistry, 13*(2), 49–50.

Jones, R., Peters, K., & Shields, E. (2007). Transform your training: Practical approaches to interactive information literacy teaching. *Journal of Information Literacy, 1*(1), 35–42.

Kaufman A., Mennin S., & Waterman, R. (1989). The New Mexico experiment: Educational innovation and institutional change. *Academic Medicine, 64*, 285–294.

Knowles, M. S. (1980). *The modern practice of adult education.* New York: Cambridge Books.

Krathwohl, D. R. (1964). The taxonomy of educational objectives: Its use in curriculum building. In C. M. Lindvall (Ed.), *Defining educational objectives* (pp. 19–36). Pittsburgh, PA: University of Pittsburgh Press.

Krathwohl, D. R. (1993). *Methods of educational and social science research: An integrated approach.* New York: Longman.

Middendorf, J., & Kalish, A. (1996). The "change-up" in lectures. *National Teaching and Learning Forum, 5*(2).

Neuman, K., & Friedman, B. (2008, November). The art of effectively facilitating professional socialization in students through affective learning. Paper presented at the Annual Program Meeting of the Council on Social Work Education, Philadelphia.

Palloff, R. M., & Pratt, K. (2011). *The excellent online instructor: Strategies for professional development.* San Francisco: Jossey-Bass.

Silberman, M. (1996). *Active learning: 101 strategies to teach any subject.* Needham Heights, MA: Allyn & Bacon.

Simpson E. (1972). *The classification of educational objectives in the psychomotor domain: The psychomotor domain* (Vol. 3). Washington, DC: Gryphon House.

ABOUT THE AUTHOR

Bruce D. Friedman, PhD, ACSW, CSWM, LCSW, is professor of social work at California State University, Bakersfield. He is the immediate past president of the board of the Network for Social Work Management and serves on the editorial boards of *Social Thought* and *Administration in Social Work*. He has a particular interest in social justice issues, integrating spirituality into practice issues, and enjoys his work with Temporary Assistance for Needy Families (TANF) and welfare-to-work recipients; people who are homeless; and people with mental illnesses and substance abuse issues, and their families. He established the Hermila Anzaldua Lecture Series and the Librado R. DeHoyos Social Work Scholarship Fund. Professor Friedman is also the author of *The Research Tool Kit: Putting It All Together* (1996, 2006), *The Ecological Perspectives Cookbook: Recipes for Social Workers* (1999), and *Social Support Networks* (1989).